Easy Phrase Book

Tourist Edition

Only the Essential Words and Phrases for Your Trip to Italy

FROM THE CREATORS OF THE
"ITALIAN HOUSE" VIDEO LESSONS

by
Andrea Macchiarulo

© **Copyright 2023 by Andrea Macchiarulo - All rights reserved.**

This book is copyright protected and intended solely for personal use. Reproduction, distribution, sale, or any other use of its content is prohibited without written permission from the author or publisher. The author and publisher assume no legal responsibility for any damages or losses resulting from the information presented in this book, either directly or indirectly. Readers should be aware that the information presented is for educational and entertainment purposes only and should not be construed as professional advice. The content has been derived from various sources, and readers should consult a licensed professional before attempting any techniques outlined in this book. By reading this book, readers acknowledge that the author is not responsible for any losses, errors, omissions, or inaccuracies resulting from the use of the information presented.

This book is adapted from the video course "Italian Course for Travellers" by Italian House. Special thanks to Jasmine and the English House of Monteverde for their advice and creation.

By purchasing this book, you gain access to exclusive bonuses! Visit the web app at https://easyitalian.netlify.app or through the QR code below, using the code provided on **page 20.**

Through the app, you'll receive:
- The video course from which this book is adapted.
- The audiobook version of the course.
- The digital version of the book, available in both English and Spanish.

If you find this book helpful, we would be immensely grateful if you could leave us a review on Amazon, as your feedback is very important to us.

Lastly, don't forget to follow us on our active social media channels by searching for **italianhouse.rome** or **italianhouserome**.

Table of Contents

INTRODUCTION 1
CHAPTER 1: MASTERING ITALIAN GREETINGS . 3
   Useful Sentences 5
   Useful Sentences Used By Italian Natives 9
CHAPTER 2: DISCOVERING NATIONALITIES AND PERSONAL INSIGHTS... 11
CHAPTER 3: EXPLORING THE ITALIAN SHOPPING EXPERIENCE 14
   Useful Sentences 17
   Useful Sentence Used By Italian Natives 21
CHAPTER 4: EMBRACING THE ITALIAN COFFEE CULTURE 24
CHAPTER 5: NAVIGATING ITALIAN TRANSPORTATION 27
   Useful Sentences 29
   Useful Sentences Used By Italian Natives 33
CHAPTER 6: UNVEILING THE ITALIAN HOSPITALITY... 39
   Useful Sentences 41
CHAPTER 7: ITALIAN DINING DEMYSTIFIED ... 49
   Useful Sentences 51
   Useful Sentences Used By Italian Natives 56
   Traditional Dishes For The Most Important Italian Regions
   57

Famous Local Wines To Pair With The Most Famous Italian Dishes 60

Brief Guide To Italian Wines 61

Useful Sentences When You Are At A Pizzeria 63

Useful Sentence Used By Italian Natives 67

Brief Guide To Italian Pizzas 68

CHAPTER 8: NAVIGATING HEALTH IN ITALY 71

Useful Sentences 74

Special And Customized Requests 78

Cultural Exchange: 85

Special Chapter : Mastering the Basics 88

The Italian Alphabet: 88

Seasons: 89

Months of the Year: 89

Days of the Week: 90

Numbers: 90

Useful Sentences & Words 91

CONCLUSION: EMBRACING YOUR ITALIAN JOURNEY 94

INTRODUCTION

The Journey Begins

The sun in Italy shone warmly on the old streets of Rome. You were in the middle of ancient ruins that had seen centuries of history. The view was like a perfect postcard, with impressive buildings, bustling cafes, and the delicious smell of coffee in the air. In this beautiful Italian moment, your adventure in Italy began—a journey into its beauty and culture.

To truly embrace the Italian experience, it is imperative to learn the language. Even mastering a few simple phrases could make a world of difference in your interactions and open the doors to new friendships and cultural experiences.

Learning a language is a journey, and like any journey, it can be enjoyable and interactive. One way to infuse your learning process with excitement is by immersing yourself in Italian culture. Going to an Italian art exhibition, listening to both traditional and modern Italian music, or watching Italian films could be a great way to get yourself used to the language.

In this way, you'll not only enhance your language skills but also get a taste of Italy's rich artistic heritage. Italy is not just a country steeped in history; it's a vibrant and alive nation, brimming with modern culture and creativity.

Now, let's talk about motivation and goal-setting. To stay motivated on your language-learning journey, it's crucial to set achievable goals and track your progress.

Set milestones for yourself—perhaps mastering a specific number of phrases each week. When you reach those goals, reward yourself. It could be as simple as treating yourself to a scoop of Italian gelato or trying an authentic Italian dish for the first time. By doing this, you'll keep your spirits high and your motivation intact.

Your journey in Italy is not just about the destination; it's about the experiences, connections, and memories you create along the way. Learning Italian basics for your trip to Italy can be both rewarding and enjoyable. Throughout our video course and the associated book, we hope you will unlock the door to unforgettable moments and connect with the Italian people on a profound level.

CHAPTER 1:
MASTERING ITALIAN GREETINGS

Imagine you've just landed at the bustling airport in Rome or Milan, ready to begin your journey through Italy. The first step is to understand the essentials of Italian greetings. Greetings are more than just words; they're the key to starting your Italian adventure on the right foot. Having these skills will be indispensable as you make your way from the airport to the heart of the city.

Greetings hold a special place in the hearts of Italians. They are less casual than what you might find in some English-speaking countries. The level of formality is something you must consider when greeting someone. Depending on the situation, you may need to address a person differently.

If you're speaking to someone you don't know, it's customary to address a man as **'signore'** and a woman as **'signora,'** while a young woman may be referred to as **'signorina**.' Now, let's explore the distinction between formal and informal greetings.

The most universal Italian greeting is **'buongiorno,'** which translates to 'good day' or 'good morning.' It's used from morning until early afternoon and can be employed both formally and informally.

When the clock strikes late afternoon or evening, '**buonasera**' becomes the phrase of choice, meaning 'good evening.' You'll use this phrase from late afternoon until nighttime.

If you're in a formal situation and want to keep it safe, use '**Salve**' to say hello. It's like saying 'Hi,' but better for formal settings. And when it's time to say goodbye, use '**Arrivederci**' to bid farewell.

In less formal situations or when greeting someone you know well, '**Ciao**' is the word you'll hear. It serves as both a casual 'hi' and 'bye.' Italians are renowned for their friendliness, so don't be surprised if even complete strangers greet you with a 'ciao' in appropriate situations.

To engage in informal greetings, you can add phrases like "**Come stai?**" (How are you?) and respond with "**Bene, grazie. E tu?**" (Fine, thank you, and you?). In more formal scenarios, you'll use "**Come sta?**" and "**Bene, grazie. E lei?**" as equivalents.

Introducing yourself is very simple in Italian. You can say, "**Piacere**," meaning 'Nice to meet you,' followed by "**Io sono**" to state your name. If someone asks your name, they'll say, "**Come ti chiami?**" (What is your name?), and you can respond with "**Mi chiamo**" (My name is...). To ask someone to repeat, use "**Scusi?**" (Excuse me?).

It's worth mentioning that Italian distinguishes between 'tu' and 'lei' to address 'you.' 'Tu' is used with people you know well or friends, while 'lei' is a form of courtesy and respect for those you don't know or those older than you. This distinction influences the way you construct sentences.

But don't worry; Italians are understanding, and your efforts to speak their language will be appreciated.
These simple phrases will help you connect with locals and make a positive first impression. So, go ahead and confidently greet and converse with the people you meet as you explore Italy.

Useful Sentences

- **Hello! / Hi!**
    - Ciao! (chyow)

- **Good morning!**
    - Buongiorno! (bwon-jyor-noh)

- **Good afternoon!**
    - Buon pomeriggio! (bwon poh-meh-ree-jjo)

- **Good evening!**
    - Buonasera! (bwon-ah-seh-rah)

- **Good night!**
    - Buonanotte! (bwon-ah-noht-teh)

- **How are you?**
    - Come stai? (koh-meh sty)

- **I'm good, thank you.**
    - Sto bene, grazie. (stoh beh-neh, graht-tsyeh)

- **What's your name?**
    - Come ti chiami? (koh-meh tee kee-ah-mee)

- **My name is [Name].**
    - Mi chiamo [Name]. (mee kee-ah-moh [Name])

- **Nice to meet you.**
    - Piacere di conoscerti. (pyah-cheh-reh dee koh-noh-shehr-tee)

- **Where are you from?**
    - Di dove sei? (dee doh-veh say)

- **I'm from [Country].**
    - Sono di [Country]. (soh-noh dee …..)

- **Do you speak English?**
    - Parli inglese? (par-lee een-glay-zeh)

- **I don't speak Italian very well.**
    - Non parlo molto bene l'italiano. (non par-loh mohl-toh beh-neh leet-ah-lyah-noh)

- **Can you help me?**
    - Puoi aiutarmi? (pwoy ah-yoo-tar-mee)

- **I'm here on vacation.**
    - Sono qui in vacanza. (soh-noh kwee een vah-chan-zah)

- **How long will you stay?**
    - Quanto tempo rimani? (kwahn-toh teem-poh ree-mah-nee)

- **I'm traveling with my family.**
    - Sto viaggiando con la mia famiglia. (stoh vee-ah-jjan-doh kon lah mee-ah fah-meel-yah)

- **I'm traveling alone.**
    - Sto viaggiando da solo. (stoh vee-ah-jjan-doh dah soh-loh)

- **I'm on a business trip.**
    - Sono qui per lavoro. (soh-noh kwee pehr lah-voh-roh)

- **This is my friend, [Name].**
    - Questo è il mio amico, [Name]. (kweh-stoh eh eel mee-oh ah-mee-coh, [Name])

- **What do you do for a living?**
    - Che lavoro fai? (keh lah-voh-roh fy)

- **Goodbye! / Bye!**
    - Arrivederci! / Ciao! (ahr-ree-veh-dehr-chee / chyow)

- **See you later!**
    - Ci vediamo dopo! (chee veh-dee-ah-moh doh-poh)

- **Have a good day!**
    - Buona giornata! (bwon-ah jyor-nah-tah)

- **Thank you for your help.**
    - Grazie per il tuo aiuto. (graht-tsyeh pehr eel two-oh ah-yoo-toh)

- **Excuse me, are you [Name]?**
    - Scusi, lei è [Name]? (skoo-see, lay eh [Name])

- **Pleased to meet you too.**
    - Piacere mio. (pyah-cheh-reh mee-oh)

- **Sorry, I didn't understand.**
    - Scusa, non ho capito. (skoo-sah, non oh kah-pee-toh)

- **Can you repeat that?**
    - Puoi ripetere? (pwoy ree-peh-teh-reh)

Useful Sentences Used By Italian Natives

- **What's new?**
    - Che novità? (keh noh-vee-tah?)

- **Long time no see!**
    - È un sacco che non ci vediamo! (eh oon sahk-koh keh non chee veh-dee-ah-moh!)

- **You haven't changed a bit!**
    - Non sei cambiato per niente! (non say kam-bee-ah-toh pehr nee-en-teh)

- **How's everything going?**
    - Come va? (koh-meh vah?)

- **Let's catch up soon!**
    - Sentiamoci! (fah-chyah-moh-chee)

- **How's the family?**
    - Come sta la famiglia? (koh-meh stah lah fah-meel-yah?)

- **It's been ages!**
    - È una vita! (eh oo-nah vee-tah!)

- **Did you cut your hair? It looks good!**
    - Ti sei tagliato i capelli? Stanno bene! (tee say tah-glyah-toh ee kah-pel-lee? stahn-noh beh-neh!)

- **You always have such a good vibe!**
  - Hai sempre un'aria così positiva! (hy sem-pray oon-ah-ree-ah koh-zee poh-zee-tee-vah!)

CHAPTER 2:
DISCOVERING NATIONALITIES AND PERSONAL INSIGHTS

When we travel, we meet many people, so it's important to know how to handle simple personal conversations. Talking about nationalities and age is key to making meaningful connections, especially in Italy, a melting pot of cultures. We will explore the world of nationalities and personal questions, giving you the tools to talk comfortably with the locals.

Let's start by mastering the art of asking, "Where are you from?". This is key, and in Italian, it's expressed as **"Di dove sei?"**. When someone asks you this question, you can respond with "**Sono di [city],**" which means "I am from [city], as in "**Sono di Boston"** ("I am from Boston").

Remember, Italian nationalities have varying endings, like "**italiano**" for males and "**italiana**" for females, so paying attention to these nuances is crucial.

As we progress, let's shift our focus to another fundamental aspect: asking someone's age. In Italian, the phrase **"Quanti anni hai?"** translates to "How old are you?" Responding to this query involves stating your age, such as **"Ho venti anni,"** meaning "I am twenty years old."

If you familiarize yourself with numbers in Italian, you'll be able to understand and get yourself understood, in various contexts. In Italian culture, discussing nationalities and age is more than a simple exchange; it's a way of expressing genuine interest and building authentic connections. Italians often engage in friendly conversations, valuing the personal connections that arise from such exchanges. When presented with questions about your background or age, embracing the conversation with an open heart can lead to beautiful moments you will remember. Usually, people aren't bothered if you ask them their age, even though traditionally, it wasn't considered appropriate to ask an adult woman her age.

A crucial point to note is the distinct pronunciation of vowels in the Italian language, which significantly influences how countries and nationalities are articulated. Pay attention to the clear sounds of vowels, such as A, E, I, O, and U, as they can alter the pronunciation of certain words. Here's a table summarizing the information about the distinct pronunciation of vowels in the Italian language.

Vowel	Pronunciation in Italian	Example
A	Clear and open 'ah' sound	America (ah-MEH-ree-kah)
E	Pronounced as 'ay'	Edimburgo (ay-deem-BOOR-goh)
I	Sounds like 'ee'	Irlanda (eer-LAHN-dah)
O	Pronounced as 'oh'	Olanda (oh-LAHN-dah)
U	Similar to 'oo'	Australia (ah-OO-strah-lee-ah)

In conclusion, you now have the foundation to connect more meaningfully with Italians by discussing nationalities and asking about age. These are essential skills to enhance your interactions and better understand Italian culture. Continue to explore and embrace the Italian language and culture.

CHAPTER 3:
EXPLORING THE ITALIAN SHOPPING EXPERIENCE

Italy is renowned for its unique shopping experiences, offering everything from high-end boutiques to artisan shops and bustling markets. Whether you're exploring quaint boutiques, local markets, or supermarkets, knowing how to navigate the shopping landscape in Italian will prove immensely useful.

Cities like Rome and Milan are worldwide known for the unique shopping experience they can offer, so let's explore the shopping experience in those cities.

On one hand, there is Rome. In the city center, there's a well-known street called Via del Corso, filled with busy shops featuring both international and Italian fashion brands. As you walk along this historic street, you can practice your Italian by asking about the prices of stylish Italian shoes or finding out where the nearest boutique is. When you find the ideal Italian leather bag, you can confidently say, "**Mi piace, lo prendo**" ("I like it! I'll take it,") and complete your purchase. If you're not sure and need time to think, you can say "**Ci penserò**" ("I'll think about it").

Milan, on the other hand, is considered the fashion capital of the world and offers an array of shopping opportunities. In the high-end boutiques of the Quadrilatero della Moda, you can ask for assistance in Italian and explore the latest fashion collections. If you're at a Milanese market, like the famous Mercato di Porta Genova, you can inquire about prices for fresh produce and regional delicacies. Practice your Italian by asking the vendor, "**Quanto costa?**" when selecting local olive oil or artisanal cheese. As you native the bustling streets of Milan, you'll find that connecting with the locals through the Italian language enhances your shopping experience.

Fancy shops and boutiques aren't the only shopping options available in Italy. If you're looking for something more affordable and simple, check one of the many "bancarelle" in town.

A "**bancarella**" is essentially a street stall or market stand where local vendors set up shop to sell a variety of goods. You'll find "bancarelle" in bustling Italian piazzas, local markets, and even at special events or festivals. These delightful stalls offer a diverse range of products, from artisan crafts and souvenirs to fresh produce, clothing, and accessories. It's an excellent place to hunt for one-of-a-kind, handcrafted items, sample regional specialties, or find unique mementos to remember your trip by.

Next, let's explore shopping in a supermarket, which is convenient for everyday shopping needs. Here are phrases specific to supermarket shopping:

To ask where to find a specific product, say "**Dove posso trovare...?**" which means "Where can I find...?". When you need a particular item, use "**Mi serve...**" followed by the item's name. For example, "**Mi serve del latte**" means "I need some milk."
When buying items that are sold by quantity, the vendor might ask, "**Quanto ne vuoi?**" which means "How much do you want?" To respond, say "**Voglio...,**" which means "I want..." followed by the quantity you desire.

Now, after selecting your items, it's time to pay. Here's how to handle the payment process.
To ask for the total cost of your purchases, use "**Quanto costa in totale?**" meaning "How much is it in total?". If you want to know if you can pay with a credit card, ask "**Posso pagare con carta di credito?**" If not, the salesperson might say "**solo contanti**," which means "only cash." To request a receipt, say "**Ricevuta, per favore.**"

Shopping in Italy is more than just a transaction; it's a social experience. Italians appreciate friendly interactions and may engage in small talk while you shop. Embrace the opportunity to connect with locals and immerse yourself in the vibrant atmosphere.

Useful Sentences

- **I'm just looking, thank you.**
    - Sto solo guardando, grazie. (stoh soh-loh gwahr-dahn-doh, graht-tsyeh)

- **Do you have this in a size [size]?**
    - Avete questo nella taglia [size]? (ah-veh-teh kwehs-toh nehl-lah tah-lyah [size]?)

- **Where are the fitting rooms?**
    - Dove sono i camerini? (doh-veh soh-noh ee kah-meh-ree-nee?)

- **How much does this cost?**
    - Quanto costa questo? (kwahn-toh koh-stah kwehs-toh?)

- **Is this on sale?**
    - È in saldo questo? (eh een sahl-doh kwehs-toh?)

- **Can I try this on?**
    - Posso provarlo? (pohs-soh proh-vahr-loh?)

- **Do you have this in another color?**
    - Avete questo in un altro colore? (ah-veh-teh kwehs-toh een oon ahl-troh koh-loh-ray?)

- **I'm looking for a [type of clothing, e.g., dress].**
    - Sto cercando un/una [type of clothing, e.g., dress]. (stoh cher-kahn-doh oon/oonah [type])

- **Do you have any jeans?**
    - Avete dei jeans? (ah-veh-teh day jeans?)

- **Is this the latest collection?**
    - È la nuova collezione? (eh lah noo-oh-vah kohl-leh-tsyoh-neh?)

- **These shoes are too tight.**
    - Queste scarpe sono troppo strette. (kwehs-teh skahr-peh soh-noh trohp-poh streht-teh)

- **Do you offer alterations?**
    - Fate le modifiche? (fah-teh leh moh-dee-fee-keh?)

- **Can I return or exchange this if it doesn't fit?**
    - Posso restituire o scambiare se non va bene? (pohs-soh reh-stee-too-ee-ray oh skahm-byah-reh seh non vah beh-neh?)

- **Do you have a larger/smaller size?**
    - Avete una taglia più grande/piccola? (ah-veh-teh oonah tah-lyah pyoo grahn-deh/peek-koh-lah?)

- **This is too expensive. Can you give a discount?**
    - È troppo caro. Potete fare uno sconto? (eh trohp-poh kah-roh. poh-teh-teh fah-ray oonoh skohn-toh?)

- **Do you have a loyalty card or any ongoing promotions?**
    - Avete una carta fedeltà o delle promozioni in corso? (ah-veh-teh oonah kahr-tah feh-del-tah oh del-leh proh-moh-tsyoh-nee een kohr-soh?)

- **I'll take it.**
    - Lo prendo. (loh prehn-doh)

- **Where can I pay?**
    - Dove posso pagare? (doh-veh pohs-soh pah-gah-ray?)

- **I'm looking for something casual/elegant.**
    - Cerco qualcosa di casual/elegante. (cher-koh kwahl-koh-zah dee kahz-oo-ahl/el-eh-gahn-teh)

- **Are these real leather?**
    - Sono di vera pelle? (soh-noh dee veh-rah pahl-leh?)

- **Do you have matching accessories?**
    - Avete accessori abbinati? (ah-veh-teh ahk-sess-oh-ree ahb-bee-nah-tee?)

- **Can I see that item in the window?**
    - Posso vedere quell'articolo in vetrina? (pohs-soh veh-deh-ray kwel-lahr-tee-koh-loh een veh-tree-nah?)

- **Do you gift wrap?**
    - Fate confezioni regalo? (fah-teh kohn-feh-tsyoh-nee reh-gah-loh?)

- **I like this, but do you have something similar in a different material?**
    - Mi piace questo, ma avete qualcosa di simile in un altro materiale? (mee pyah-cheh kwehs-toh, mah ah-veh -teh kwahl-koh-zah dee see-mee-leh een oon ahl-troh mah-teh-ryah-leh?)

- **When will you have new stock?**
    - Quando avrete nuovi arrivi? (kwahn-doh ah-vreh-teh noo-oh-vee ah-ree-vee?)

App Code : 79367

- **Do you have a catalog I can look at?**
    - Avete un catalogo che posso guardare? (ah-veh-teh oon kah-tah-loh-goh keh pohs-soh gwahr-dah-ray?)

- **This seems defective. Do you have another one?**
    - Questo sembra difettoso. Ne avete un altro? (kwehs-toh sem-brah dee-feht-toh-soh. neh ah-veh-teh oon ahl-troh?)

- **Are these the only designs you have?**
    - Sono gli unici modelli che avete? (soh-noh lyee oo-nee-chee moh-del-lee keh ah-veh-teh?)

- **I'd like to see more options.**
    - Vorrei vedere più opzioni. (vor-ray veh-deh-ray pyoo op-tsyoh-nee)

Useful Sentence Used By Italian Natives

- **Can you recommend any accessories to go with this?**
    - Puoi consigliare degli accessori che si abbinano a questo? (pwoy kon-seelyah-reh deyee ahk-ses-soh-ree keh see ahb-bee-nah-no ah kwehs-toh?)

- **I'm not sure about the size. Can I exchange it if it doesn't fit?**
    - Non sono sicuro/a della taglia. Posso scambiarlo se non va bene? (non soh-noh see-koo-roh/ah deyee-ah tah-lyah. pohs-soh skahm-byar-loh seh non vah beh-neh?)

- **This dress is for a special occasion. Do you have any similar options?**
    - Questo vestito è per un'occasione speciale. Avete delle opzioni simili? (kweh-stoh vehs-tee-toh eh pehr oon oh-kah-syoh-neh speh-chah-leh. ah-veh-teh deyee op-tsyoh-nee see-mee-lee?)

- **I'm on a budget. Can you show me more affordable options?**
    - Ho un budget limitato. Puoi mostrarmi opzioni più economiche? (oh oon boo-jet lee-mee-tah-toh. pwoy mohr-strahr-mee op-tsyoh-nee pyoo eh-koh-noh-mee-keh?)

- **This shirt is a bit loose. Do you have a smaller size?**
    - Questa camicia è un po' larga. Avete una taglia più piccola? (kweh-stah kah-mee-chah eh oon poh lahr-gah. ah-veh-teh oo-nah tah-lyah pyoo peek-koh-lah?)

- **I'm looking for something elegant for a formal event.**
    - Cerco qualcosa di elegante per un evento formale. (cher-koh kwahl-koh-zah dee el-eh-gahn-teh pehr oon eh-ven-toh for-mah-leh.)

- **Can I return this if I change my mind after purchasing?**
    - Posso restituire questo se cambio idea dopo l'acquisto? (pohs-soh reh-stee-tw-e-reh kweh-stoh seh kam-byoh ee-deh doh-po lah-kwee-stoh?)

- **I like the style, but I'm not sure about the color.**
    - Mi piace lo stile, ma non sono sicuro/a del colore. (mee pyah-cheh loh stee-leh, mah non soh-noh see-koo-roh/ah del koh-loh-reh.)

- **Is there a discount if I purchase more than one item?**
    - C'è uno sconto se compro più di un articolo? (cheh oo-noh skohn-toh seh kohm-proh pyoo dee oon ar-tee-koh-loh?)

- **I need a casual outfit for everyday wear.**
    - Ho bisogno di un outfit casual per tutti i giorni. (oh bee-sohn-yoh dee oon out-fit kah-zoo-ahl pehr toot-tee ee jor-nee.)

CHAPTER 4:
EMBRACING THE ITALIAN COFFEE CULTURE

Italy, synonymous with a robust coffee culture, offers an unparalleled experience for enthusiasts. Ordering coffee in an Italian café is an art, a dance between tradition and personal preference. Unveiling the essentials is crucial for navigating the vibrant world of Italian cafés. Let's unravel the aromatic layers of this experience together!

Firstly, there's the classic "**caffe,**" or espresso. Brace yourself for its robust flavor; however, if you seek a milder version, consider the "caffe lungo," an espresso with a bit more water, though distinct from American coffee. True to their coffee heritage, Italians often forgo sugar, but the choice is yours.

Moving on, the iconic "**cappuccino**" graces the morning routines of many Italians. Paired with a "**cornetto**" in Rome or a "**brioche**" in the north, it's a breakfast delight. While it's customary to refrain from ordering a cappuccino after dinner in a restaurant, don't hesitate to savor one in a local "**bar**" or cafe in English.

For those seeking a unique flavor, the "**caffe al Ginseng**" offers a sweet and energizing alternative. Available in "**tazza piccola**" (espresso size) or "**tazza grande**" (cappuccino size), it's a personal favorite for many.

If you prefer a gentler and longer coffee experience, go for the "**Americano**." Here it's made by adding hot water to espresso, giving it a taste similar to drip coffee.

Before ordering, remember to pay at the "**cassa**" or cash desk, keeping the receipt or "**scontrino**" handy for the barista, and state your seating preference. If you opt to stand at the counter, you might say, "**Al banco, per favore.**" If not, say "al tavolo" ("at the table"). Some cafes have different prices if you have your coffee at the counter or at the table, so you better make sure of it before paying.

Politeness is appreciated, so express what you would like by saying **"vorrei"** (I would like) and conclude with "**per favore**" (please). For instance, "**Vorrei un cappuccino, per favore**" (I would like a cappuccino, please).

Finally, we'll describe two very famous "bar" in Italy: "Sant'Eustachio II il Caffè" in Rome and "Bar Luce" in Milan.

"Sant'Eustachio Il Caffè," established in 1938 near the Pantheon in Rome, is a renowned and iconic bar celebrated for its traditional coffee-making methods. This historic cafe is particularly famous for its "gran caffe," an espresso with a distinctive roasting process that imparts a touch of sweetness without the need for sugar. A favorite among locals and tourists,

Sant'Eustachio exudes classic Roman charm with its marble counters and wooden decor, providing an authentic and timeless experience. Beyond its exceptional coffee, the bar has become a symbol of Rome's coffee culture, preserving heritage and contributing significantly to the city's culinary and cultural legacy.

Located in the Fondazione Prada complex in Milan, "**Bar Luce**" is a unique and renowned bar designed by the acclaimed filmmaker Wes Anderson. Opened in 2015, Bar Luce is characterized by its whimsical and retro aesthetic, reminiscent of Anderson's distinctive cinematic style. The pastel-colored decor, vintage jukebox, and carefully curated mid-century furniture create an atmosphere that transports patrons into a Wes Anderson film. While known for its cinematic ambiance, Bar Luce also offers a delightful menu of pastries, sandwiches, and beverages. This iconic bar has become a popular destination not only for its connection to the arts but also for providing visitors with a one-of-a-kind visual and culinary experience in the heart of Milan.

The Italian coffee culture transcends a mere beverage; it's a social interaction, an integral part of daily life. As you navigate this caffeinated journey, take a moment to savor not just the coffee but the ambiance, the conversations, and the rich tapestry of Italian culture woven into every cup.

CHAPTER 5:
NAVIGATING ITALIAN TRANSPORTATION

Exploring Italy is both enchanting and sometimes a bit challenging, creating a beautiful yet complex adventure. This beauty comes with challenges in navigating a diverse transportation system, where efficiency varies by region. Moving from busy metros to small village buses adds depth to the journey, revealing the true essence of Italy in spontaneity, vibrant local life, and unexpected encounters.

Understanding how these diverse transportation modes function in Italy ensures a smoother, more enjoyable travel experience, allowing you to explore the country's beauty with ease. Here is a concise explanation of the main forms of transportation in Italy.

Autobus (Bus): Buses, or "autobus" in Italian, form an extensive transportation network across Italy, connecting regions, cities, and remote villages. While cost-effective, their efficiency may vary, especially during peak hours. Checking with locals for information on reliability and schedules is advisable.

Pullman (Coaches): Pullman refers to coaches, which cover extended routes and connecting cities. Though slower than trains, they are generally reliable and cost-effective. Various apps provide information on coach options and prices.

Metro (Subway/Underground): Found in major cities, the metro offers an efficient way to navigate urban landscapes, especially city centers. In summer, metros can be crowded, and caution is advised regarding pickpockets.

Treni (Trains): Trains, operated by companies like Trenitalia and Italo, are a vital part of Italy's transportation system, providing both high-speed and local options. The rail network is generally efficient, connecting major cities and towns for a scenic and comfortable exploration.

Traghetto (Ferry): Traghetti, or ferries, play a crucial role in regions with numerous islands, providing scenic routes between coastal destinations.

Locating places, bus stops, and train stations is not easy. When asking for directions, polite phrases like "**Scusi, dov'è...?**" or "**Come arrivo...?**" are essential. Key words like "**Vicino**" for near and "**Lontano**" for far help understand distances. Keep in mind also that "**A sinistra, a destra, dritto**" signifies left, right, and straight on.

In bustling cities like Milan or Rome, getting lost can happen. Seeking help politely with "**Mi può aiutare?**" meaning "Can you help me?" is valuable.

For ticket-related inquiries, use phrases like "**Quando parte il prossimo autobus/treno?**" for departure times, "**Quanto costa il biglietto?**" for ticket prices, and "**Vorrei un biglietto per...**" for requesting a ticket to a specific destination.

Remember to validate your ticket before boarding when traveling by train or bus, using designated machines to avoid fines. Some cities even allow direct credit card payments for added convenience.

In summary, exploring Italy's varied transportation system adds an intriguing layer to the travel adventure. Although the country's beauty is unparalleled, the challenges posed by its diverse transit systems enhance the journey. Embracing spontaneity, connecting with vibrant local life, and cherishing unexpected encounters capture the essence of the Italian travel experience. With a better grasp of transportation details and key phrases, every twist and turn becomes a crucial part of an unforgettable adventure through the heart of Italy.

Useful Sentences

- **Where is the bus station?**
    - Dov'è la stazione degli autobus? (doh-veh lah stah-tsyoh-neh day-lee ow-toh-boos)

- **How much is a ticket to...?**
  - Quanto costa un biglietto per...? (kwan-toh koh-stah oon beel-yet-toh pehr)

- **Where can I buy a ticket?**
  - Dove posso comprare un biglietto? (doh-veh pohs-soh kom-prah-reh oon beel-yet-toh)

- **When is the next train to...?**
  - Quando è il prossimo treno per...? (kwan-doh eh eel prohs-see-moh treh-noh pehr)

- **Does this bus go to...?**
  - Questo autobus va a...? (kweh-stoh ow-toh-boos vah ah)ow-toh-boos vah ah)

- **I need a taxi.**
  - Ho bisogno di un taxi. (oh bee-zoh-nyoh dee oon tah-xee)

- **Take me to this address, please.**
  - Portami a questo indirizzo, per favore. (por-tah-mee ah kweh-stoh een-dee-ree-tsoh, pehr fah-vo-reh)

- **How far is... from here?**
  - Quanto dista... da qui? (kwan-toh dees-tah dah kwee)

- **Is it within walking distance?**
    - È raggiungibile a piedi? (eh rah-joon-jee-bee-leh ah pyeh-dee)

- **Can you show me on the map?**
    - Puoi mostrarmi sulla mappa? (pwoy mohs-tar-mee sool-lah mahp-pah)

- **What time does the last train/bus leave?**
    - A che ora parte l'ultimo treno/autobus? (ah keh oh-rah par-teh lool-tee-moh treh-noh/ow-toh-boos)

- **Is there a subway station nearby?**
    - C'è una stazione della metropolitana vicino? (cheh oonah stah-tsyoh-neh del-lah meh-troh-poh-lee-tah-nah vee-chee-noh)

- **Where can I rent a car?**
    - Dove posso noleggiare una macchina? (doh-veh pohs-soh noh-leh-jyah-reh oonah makh-kee-nah)

- **How much is the fare?**
    - Quanto è la tariffa? (kwan-toh eh lah tah-ree-fah)

- **I'd like to go to the airport.**
    - Vorrei andare all'aeroporto. (vor-ray ahn-dah-reh al-lah-eh-roh-por-toh)

- **Is there a direct line to...?**
  - C'è una linea diretta per...? (cheh oonah lee-eh-nah dee-reht-tah pehr)

- **Can I have a timetable/schedule?**
  - Posso avere un orario? (pohs-soh ah-veh-reh oon oh-rah-ryo)

- **I'm lost.**
  - Mi sona perso/a. (mee soh-noh pehr-soh/ah)

- **Which way to...?**
  - In quale direzione per...? (een kwah-leh dee-rehk-tsyoh-neh pehr)

- **Stop here, please.**
  - Fermati qui, per favore. (fehr-mah-tee kwee, pehr fah-vo-reh)

- **Is parking allowed here?**
  - È permesso parcheggiare qui? (eh pehr-mehs-soh par-keh-jyah-reh kwee)

- **Can I get a day pass?**
  - Posso avere un abbonamento giornaliero? (pohs-soh ah-veh-reh oon ahb-boh-nah-men-toh johr-nah-lee-eh-roh)

- **Which platform does the train leave from?**
  - Da quale binario parte il treno? (dah kwah-leh been-ah-ryo par-teh eel treh-noh)

- **I missed my stop.**
  - Ho perso la mia fermata. (oh pehr-soh lah myah fehr-mah-tah)

- **When is the next departure?**
  - Quando è la prossima partenza? (kwan-doh eh lah prohs-see-mah par-ten-tsah)

- **Is this seat free?**
  - Questo posto è libero? (kweh-stoh poh-stoh eh lee-beh-roh)

- **Does this road lead to...?**
  - Questa strada porta a...? (kweh-stah strah-dah por-tah ah)

- **How long is the journey?**
  - Quanto dura il viaggio? (kwan-toh doo-rah eel vee-ahj-joh)

Useful Sentences Used By Italian Natives

- **Where is the main square?**
  - Dov'è la piazza principale? (doh-veh lah pyah-tsah preen-chee-pah-leh)

- **Can you recommend a good museum?**
    - Puoi consigliarmi un buon museo? (pwoy kon-see-lyar-mee oon bwon moo-zeh-oh)

- **How do I get to the Colosseum?**
    - Come arrivo al Colosseo? (koh-meh ah-ree-voh al Koh-lohs-say-oh)

- **Are there guided tours available?**
    - Ci sono visite guidate disponibili? (chee soh-noh veez-ee-teh gwee-dah-teh dees-poh-nee-bee-lee)

- **What are the opening hours?**
    - Quali sono gli orari di apertura? (kwah-lee soh-noh lyee oh-rah-ree dee ah-pehr-too-rah)

- **How much is the entrance fee?**
    - Quanto costa il biglietto d'ingresso? (kwan-toh koh-stah eel beel-yet-toh deen-grehs-soh)

- **Where is the nearest tourist information center?**
    - Dov'è il centro informazioni turistiche più vicino? (doh-veh eel chen-troh een-for-mah-tsyoh-nee too-ree-stee-kei pyoo vee-chee-noh)

- **Is it safe to walk here at night?**
    - È sicuro camminare qui di notte? (eh see-koo-roh kahm-mee-nah-reh kwee dee noht-teh)

- **I'm looking for a local market.**
    - Sto cercando un mercato locale. (stoh cher-kahn-doh oon mehr-kah-toh loh-kah-leh)

- **Can you suggest a good place to take photos?**
    - Puoi suggerirmi un buon posto per fare foto? (pwoy soo-jehr-mee oon bwon poh-stoh pehr fah-reh fo-toh)

- **Where can I find a traditional restaurant?**
    - Dove posso trovare un ristorante tradizionale? (doh-veh pohs-soh troh-vah-reh oon ree-stoh-rahnt-teh trah-dee-tsyoh-nah-leh)

- **Is there a local festival or event happening?**
    - C'è un festival o un evento locale in corso? (cheh oon feh-stee-val oh oon eh-ven-toh loh-kah-leh een kor-soh)

- **What's the best way to explore the city?**
    - Qual è il miglior modo per esplorare la città? (kwal eh eel mee-lyor moh-doh pehr es-ploh-rah-reh lah cheet-tah)

- **Is there a city map available?**
    - C'è una mappa della città disponibile? (cheh oonah mahp-pah del-lah cheet-tah dees-poh-nee-bee-leh)

- **Where can I buy souvenirs?**
    - Dove posso comprare souvenir? (doh-veh pohs-soh kom-prah-reh soo-veh-neer)

- **Are there any historical sites nearby?**
    - Ci sono siti storici nelle vicinanze? (chee soh-noh see-tee stoh-ree-chee nel-leh vee-chee-nahn-tseh)

- **I'd like to go on a boat tour.**
    - Vorrei fare un giro in barca. (vor-ray fah-reh oon jee-roh een bar-kah)

- **Is there a good viewpoint around?**
    - C'è un buon punto panoramico nelle vicinanze? (cheh oon bwon poon-toh pah-noh-rah-mee-koh nel-leh vee-chee-nahn-tseh)

- **Are there walking tours of the city?**
    - Ci sono tour a piedi della città? (chee soh-noh toor ah pyeh-dee del-lah cheet-tah)

- **Where is the local nightlife?**
    - Dov'è la vita notturna locale? (doh-veh lah vee-tah noh-toor-nah loh-kah-leh)

- **Can you recommend any cultural events?**
    - Puoi consigliarmi qualche evento culturale? (pwoy kon-see-lyar-mee kwal-ke eh-ven-toh kool-too-rah-leh)

- **Are there any public parks or gardens?**
    - Ci sono parchi pubblici o giardini? (chee soh-noh par-kee poob-blee-chee oh jyar-dee-nee)

- **What is this building?**
    - Cos'è questo edificio? (kohz-eh kweh-stoh ed-ee-fycho)

- **Are there any famous landmarks I should visit?**
    - Ci sono punti di riferimento famosi che dovrei visitare? (chee soh-noh poon-tee dee ree-fehr-ee-men-toh fah-moh-see keh doh-vray vee-zee-tah-reh)

- **Where can I find a local guide?**
    - Dove posso trovare una guida locale? (doh-veh pohs-soh troh-vah-reh oonah gwee-dah loh-kah-leh)

- **How old is this monument?**
    - Quanti anni ha questo monumento? (kwan-tee an-nee hah kweh-stoh moh-noo-men-toh)

- **Is there an entrance fee for this place?**
    - C'è un costo d'ingresso per questo posto? (cheh oon koh-stoh deen-grehs-soh pehr kweh-stoh poh-stoh)

- **What local delicacies should I try?**
    - Quali specialità locali dovrei provare? (kwah-lee speh-chyah-lee-tah loh-kah-lee doh-vray proh-vah-reh)

- **Where can I find street performers or local music?**
    - Dove posso trovare artisti di strada o musica locale? (doh-veh pohs-soh troh-vah-reh ar-tees-tee dee strah-dah oh moo-zee-kah loh-kah-leh)

CHAPTER 6:
UNVEILING THE ITALIAN HOSPITALITY

As you embark on your Italian journey, the anticipation of exploring its enchanting landscapes and rich history is met with the reality of settling into your chosen accommodations. Navigating the intricacies of Italian hotels is an essential part of your adventure. This chapter will guide you through the hotel check-in process and equip you with the knowledge to make your stay as comfortable as possible.

Before delving into the check-in process, let's familiarize ourselves with some essential hotel-related terms.

The first thing to know is how to say hotel; in Italian, it is called "**albergo**." However, the word hotel is still well understood by Italians. The area where you'll check in and seek assistance throughout your stay is "**la reception**." Then you'll probably be asked if you have a reservation or "**prenotazione**," so ensure you have your reservation details handy during check-in.

After finalizing the check-in procedure, you'll be brought to "**la camera**," the room where you'll be staying in. Specify the type of room you reserved, like '**una camera singola**' for a single room or '**una camera doppia**' for a double room. Don't forget to ask for "'**la chiave**," the key to your room.

Upon arriving at your chosen hotel, initiating the check-in process requires a few key phrases; here are some useful ones.

- **Buongiorno, ho una prenotazione**. (Good morning, I have a reservation.)This phrase informs the receptionist that you have a reservation, kicking off the check-in process.

- **Vorrei fare il check-in, per favore**. (I would like to check in, please.)Express your desire to check in with this polite phrase, prompting the receptionist to guide you through the process.

- **Mi può dare la chiave della camera?** (Can you give me the room key?)When you're ready to receive your room key, this question will ensure you have access to your accommodation.

Hotels are not only a place to rest but also somewhere to relax and switch off from our usual routine. Hotel amenities are everyone's favorite as we get special treats we are not used to getting.

Having breakfast in a hotel is a brilliant way to kick in a busy day wandering around any Italian city. Ask "**Dove si serve la colazione?**" (Where is breakfast served?) to locate the breakfast area or restaurant.
Inquire about meal times to plan your day accordingly by saying "**A che ora è la colazione/pranzo/cena?**" (What time is breakfast/lunch/dinner?)

Nowadays, every hotel has free Wi-Fi available, in order to make sure of it, say "**C'è il Wi-Fi gratuito?**" (Is there free Wi-Fi?).

Finally, keep in mind that floors in Italy are numbered in a different way: the ground floor is called '**Piano terra,**' followed by '**primo piano**' (first floor), '**secondo piano**' (second floor), and so on. Pay attention to these terms when locating your room.

As this chapter concludes, envision yourself confidently navigating the intricacies of Italian hotels. The doors to a comfortable stay are wide open, and your Italian adventure continues. **Buona permanenza!**

Useful Sentences

- **I have a reservation under [name].**
    - Ho una prenotazione a nome [name]. (oh oonah preh-noh-tah-tsyoh-neh ah noh-meh [name])

- **Do you have any rooms available?**
    - Avete camere disponibili? (ah-veh-teh kah-meh-reh dees-poh-nee-bee-lee?)

- **I'd like to book a room for [number] nights.**
    - Vorrei prenotare una camera per [number] notti. (vor-ray preh-noh-tah-ray oonah kah-meh-rah pehr [number] noht-tee)

- **Can I see the room first?**
    - Posso vedere la camera prima? (pohs-soh veh-deh-ray lah kah-meh-rah pree-mah?)

- **Is breakfast included?**
    - La colazione è inclusa? (lah koh-lah-tsyoh-neh eh een-kloo-sah?)

- **What is the check-out time?**
    - A che ora è il check-out? (ah keh oh-rah eh eel check-out?)

- **Do you offer room service?**
    - Offrite il servizio in camera? (oh-freet-teh eel sehr-vee-tsyoh in kah-meh-rah?)

- **I need an extra towel/pillow.**
    - Ho bisogno di un asciugamano/cuscino in più. (oh bee-sohn-yoh dee oon ah-shoo-gah-mah-noh/koos-chee-noh een pwee)
- **Is there Wi-Fi in the room?**
    - C'è Wi-Fi nella camera? (cheh wee-fee nehl-lah kah-meh-rah?)

- **How much is it per night?**
    - Quanto costa a notte? (kwahn-toh koh-stah ah noht-teh?)

- **Is there a safe in the room?**
    - C'è una cassaforte nella camera? (cheh oonah kahs-sah-for-teh nehl-lah kah-meh-rah?)

- **I'd like a room with a view.**
    - Vorrei una camera con vista. (vor-ray oonah kah-meh-rah kohn vees-tah)

- **Do you have a shuttle service to the airport?**
    - Avete un servizio navetta per l'aeroporto? (ah-veh-teh oon sehr-vee-tsyoh nah-veht-tah pehr lair-oh-por-toh?)

- **I need to extend my stay.**
    - Devo prolungare il mio soggiorno. (deh-voh proh-loon-gah-ray eel mee-oh soh-jyohr-noh)

- **Can I have a wake-up call at [time]?**
    - Potete svegliarmi alle [time]? (poh-teh-teh svehl-jyahr-mee ah-lleh [time]?)
- **The air conditioning isn't working.**
    - L'aria condizionata non funziona. (lah-ree-ah kohn-dee-tsyoh-nah-tah non foon-tsyoh-nah)

- **Where is the gym/pool?**
    - Dov'è la palestra/piscina? (doh-veh lah pah-lehs-trah/pee-shee-nah?)

- **I lost my room key.**
    - Ho perso la chiave della camera. (oh pehr-soh lah kyah-veh del-lah kah-meh-rah)

- **Do you offer laundry service?**
    - Offrite il servizio di lavanderia? (oh-freet-teh eel sehr-vee-tsyoh dee lah-vahn-deh-ree-ah?)

- **Are pets allowed?**
    - Gli animali sono ammessi? (lyee ah-nee-mah-lee soh-noh ahm-mehs-see?)

- **What time is breakfast served?**
    - A che ora servite la colazione? (ah keh oh-rah sehr-vee-teh lah koh-lah-tsyoh-neh?)

- **Is there a minibar in the room?**
    - C'è un minibar nella camera? (cheh oon mee-nee-bar nehl-lah kah-meh-rah?)

- **Can I get a different room?**
    - Posso avere una camera diversa? (pohs-soh ah-veh-ray oonah kah-meh-rah dee-vehr-sah?)

- **How do I use the safe?**
    - Come si usa la cassaforte? (koh-meh see oo-sah lah kahs-sah-for-teh?)

- **I'd like a non-smoking room.**
    - Vorrei una camera non fumatori. (vor-ray oonah kah-meh-rah non foo-mah-toh-ree)

- **Do you have an elevator?**
    - Avete un ascensore? (ah-veh-teh oon ah-sen-soh-ray?)

- **Can I store my luggage here after check-out?**
    - Posso lasciare i miei bagagli qui dopo il check-out? (pohs-soh lah-shyah-ray ee mee-eh bah-gahl-gee kwee doh-poh eel check-out?)

- **I need a crib for my baby.**
    - Ho bisogno di una culla per il mio bambino. (oh bee-sohn-yoh dee oonah kool-lah pehr eel mee-oh bam-bee-noh)

- **Are there any nearby restaurants you'd recommend?**
    - Ci sono ristoranti nelle vicinanze che consigliate? (chee soh-noh rees-toh-rahn-

tee nehl-leh vee-chee-nahn-tseh keh kohn-see-lyah-teh?)

- **Can you call a taxi for me?**
    - Potete chiamare un taxi per me?(poh-teh-teh kyah-mah-ray oon tah-xee pehr meh?)

- **The room service forgot to clean my room.**
    - Il servizio in camera ha dimenticato di pulire la mia stanza. (eel sehr-vee-tsyoh een kah-meh-rah ah dee-mehn-tee-kah-toh dee poo-lee-reh lah mee-ah stahn-zah)

- **There's a strange smell in the bathroom.**
    - C'è un odore strano in bagno. (cheh oon oh-doh-reh strah-no een bahn-yoh)

- **The shower in my room is not working properly.**
    - La doccia nella mia camera non funziona correttamente. (lah doh-chah nehl-lah mee-ah kah-meh-rah non foon-tsyoh-nah koh-reht-tah-men-teh)

- **I have a late check-in.**
    - Ho un check-in tardivo. (oh oon check-in tahr-dee-voh)

- **I would like an extra blanket.**
    - Vorrei una coperta in più. (vor-ray oonah koh-pehr-tah een pyoo)

- **Is there a business center in the hotel?**
    - C'è un centro business nell'hotel? (cheh oon chen-troh bee-nee-ss nelly-oh-tehl?)

- **The TV remote control is not functioning.**
    - Il telecomando della TV non funziona. (eel teh-leh-koh-mahn-doh deh-lah tee veh non foon-tsyoh-nah)

- **There was a problem with my reservation.**
    - C'è stato un problema con la mia prenotazione. (cheh stah-toh oon proh-bleh-mah kon lah mee-ah preh-noh-tah-tsyoh-neh)

- **I need to check out earlier than planned.**
    - Devo fare il check-out prima di quanto previsto. (deh-voh fah-reh eel check-out pree-mah dee kwahn-toh preh-vee-stoh)

- **Can you recommend a good place to eat around here?**
    - Puoi consigliare un buon posto dove mangiare qui vicino? (pwoy kon-seelyah-reh oon bwon poh-stoh doh-veh man-jyah-reh kwee vee-chee-no?)

CHAPTER 7:
ITALIAN DINING DEMYSTIFIED

Welcome to the world of Italian food—a chapter dedicated to making your dining adventures in Italy enjoyable. In this section, we'll guide you through the basics of ordering in an Italian restaurant, helping you savor the flavors and feel confident while doing so.

To eat like a local, find a place bustling with Italians. If you're only in Italy for a short stay, a bit of research before you go and some friendly questions upon arrival can lead you to the best spots. Here is a tip: when looking for a place to have lunch or dinner, try "**trattoria**"—they're cozy and simple restaurants but serve up some seriously delicious food.

Let's start our culinary adventure by making sense of the menu:

- **Antipasti**: These are the appetizers—bruschetta, salads, or meats to kick off your meal.
- **Primi Piatti**: Think pasta, risotto, or soups. They are all included in this category.
- **Secondi Piatti**: The heavier dishes—meat, poultry, fish, or vegetarian options, sometimes with a side.
- **Contorni**: Extras to accompany your main course, like veggies, salads, or potatoes.
- **Dolci**: End your meal with something sweet, like tiramisu or panna cotta.

As soon as you get to a restaurant, you are probably going to ask for a table. Start by saying **"Un tavolo per** … " ("A table for …") adjusting the number based on your group. For instance, you could say, "**Un tavolo per due,"** if you want to ask for a table for two.

Now it's time to place your order, but before you ought to read the menu. Say **"Posso avere il menu?"** ("May I have the menu?"). After deciding the dishes you would like to try, il **cameriere** (the waiter) will ask: "**Pronti a ordinare?**" ("Ready to Order?") When you're set, reply confidently explaining the dishes you'd like to eat. Use this simple phrase **"Vorrei …"** as in "**Vorrei il vino** " ("I would like some wine").

Nowadays, many of us deal with food allergies and intolerances, therefore more and more restaurants are adapting their menus with a wider variety of food options to fulfill any possible need. To check if there are vegetarian options say "**ci sono dei piatti vegetariani?**" ("Are there vegetarian options?") In case you are dealing with food allergies, inform your waiter as soon as possible by saying "**Sono allergico a …** " ("I am allergic to…") followed by the specific allergen. Here is a practical example: "**Sono allergico al glutine**" ("I am allergic to gluten").

If you loved your meal, a simple **"Buonissimo, complimenti"** ("It's very good, congratulations") to the owner goes a long way.

Lastly, we'll dedicate some time to give some extra details about cultural differences you might find in Italian restaurants. An important one is the service charge. It's not obligatory to pay for it in Italy; it depends on the restaurant you're going to. In Italian, we refer to it as "**coperto**" and you'll usually find a note in the menu that shows how much is due for it. In order to know if the restaurant you are in asks to pay for coperto, feel free to ask your waiter. Italians love food, therefore having dinner or lunch is an occasion to relax, savor the food, and soak in the local atmosphere, so take your time and avoid rushing.

You are now equipped to navigate an Italian menu, so go ahead and dive into the rich world of Italian cuisine. Your culinary journey promises not just great meals but a deeper connection to the heart of Italy. **Buon appetito!**

Useful Sentences

- **Can I see the menu?**
    - Posso vedere il menù? (pohs-soh veh-deh-ray eel meh-noo?)
- **Do you have a table for two?**
    - Avete un tavolo per due? (ah-veh-teh oon tah-voh-loh pehr dweh?)

- **I would like to order now.**
    - Vorrei ordinare adesso. (vor-ray or-dee-nah-ray ah-dess-soh)

- **What do you recommend?**
    - Cosa mi consiglia? (koh-zah mee kon-seel-yah?)

- **Is this dish spicy?**
    - Questo piatto è piccante? (kwes-toh pyah-toh eh peek-kahn-teh?)

- **Can I get this without garlic?**
    - Posso avere questo senza aglio? (pohs-soh ah-veh-ray kwes-toh sen-zah ahl-yoh?)

- **I am vegetarian.**
    - Sono vegetariano (for males) / Sono vegetariana (for females). (soh-noh veh-jeh-tah-ree-ah-noh / soh-noh veh-jeh-tah-ree-ah-nah)

- **Do you have gluten-free options?**
    - Avete opzioni senza glutine? (ah-veh-teh op-tsyoh-nee sen-zah gloo-tee-neh?)

- **Can I have the check/bill?**
    - Posso avere il conto? (pohs-soh ah-veh-ray eel kohn-toh?)

- **Is service included?**
  - Il servizio è incluso? (eel sehr-vee-tsyoh eh een-kloo-zoh?)

- **I would like some water, please.**
  - Vorrei dell'acqua, per favore. (vor-ray dell-ah-kwah, pehr fah-voh-ray)

- **Do you have a wine list?**
  - Avete la lista dei vini? (ah-veh-teh lah lees-tah day vee-nee?)

- **I'd like a glass of red/white wine.**
  - Vorrei un bicchiere di vino rosso/bianco. (vor-ray oon beek-kyeh-ray dee vee-noh roh-ssoh/b'yan-koh)

- **The food was delicious.**
  - Il cibo era delizioso. (eel chee-boh eh-rah deh-lee-tsyoh-zoh)

- **Can I take this to go?**
  - Posso portare via questo? (pohs-soh por-tah-ray vee-ah kwes-toh?)

- **Are there any daily specials?**
  - Ci sono offerte del giorno? (chee soh-noh ohf-fehr-teh del johr-noh?)

- **I have a food allergy.**
    - Ho un'allergia alimentare. (oh oon-ahl-lair-jee-ah ah-lee-men-tah-ray)

- **How is this dish prepared?**
    - Come è preparato questo piatto? (koh-meh eh preh-pah-rah-toh kwes-toh pyah-toh?)

- **Can you make it less spicy?**
    - Potete farlo meno piccante? (poh-teh-teh fahr-loh meh-noh peek-kahn-teh?)

- **I'd like my steak medium-rare.**
    - Vorrei la mia bistecca al sangue. (vor-ray lah mee-ah bees-tehk-kah ahl sahn-gweh)

- **Do you have any vegan dishes?**
    - Avete piatti vegani? (ah-veh-teh pyah-tee veh-gah-nee?)

- **Another round of drinks, please.**
    - Un altro giro di bevande, per favore. (oon ahl-troh jee-roh dee beh-vahn-deh, pehr fah-voh-ray)

- **I'll have the same as him/her.**
    - Prenderò lo stesso di lui/lei. (pren-deh-roh loh stehs-soh dee loo-ee/lay)

- **Can we get more bread?**
    - Possiamo avere più pane? (pohs-see-ah-moh ah-veh-ray pwee pah-neh?)

- **Does this contain nuts?**
    - Questo contiene noci? (kwes-toh kohn-tyeh-neh noh-chee?)

- **I'd like a table outside.**
    - Vorrei un tavolo fuori. (vor-ray oon tah-voh-loh fwoh-ree)

- **Do you take reservations?**
    - Prendete prenotazioni? (pren-deh-teh preh-noh-tah-tsyoh-nee?)

- **Is this homemade?**
    - È fatto in casa? (eh faht-toh een kah-sah?)

- **We'd like to share this dish.**
    - Vorremmo condividere questo piatto. (vor-reh-moh kohn-dee-vee-deh-ray kwes-toh pyah-toh)

- **How long is the wait?**
    - Quanto tempo bisogna aspettare? (kwahn-toh tem-poh bee-sohn-yah ahs-peh-tah-ray?)

Useful Sentences Used By Italian Natives

- **What's the chef's special tonight?**
    - Qual è la specialità dello chef stasera? (kwal eh lah speh-chal-ee-tah del-loh shef stah-seh-rah?)

- **That dish is a must-have here.**
    - Quel piatto è un must qui. (kwel pyah-toh eh oon moost kwee)

- **This place is always packed!**
    - Questo posto è sempre pieno! (kwes-toh pohs-toh eh sem-pray pyee-noh)

- **I could eat here every day.**
    - Potrei mangiare qui ogni giorno. (poh-tray man-jyah-ray kwee oh-jnee johr-noh)

- **They have the best [dish] in town.**
    - Hanno il miglior [dish] in città. (hahn-noh eel meel-yor [dish] een chee-tah)

- **This is a hidden gem.**
    - Questo è un posto nascosto. (kwes-toh eh oon pohs-toh nah-skos-toh)

- **Let's dig in!**
    - Mangiamo! (mahn-jyah-moh)

- **That was a feast!**
    - È stato un banchetto! (eh stah-toh oon bahn-ket-toh)

- **This place never disappoints.**
    - Questo posto non delude mai. (kwes-toh pohs-toh non deh-loo-deh my)

- **You've got to try this!**
    - Devi assolutamente provare questo! (deh-vee ahs-soh-loo-tah-men-teh proh-vah-ray kwes-toh)

Traditional Dishes For The Most Important Italian Regions

- **Roma:** Cacio e Pepe (kah-choh eh peh-peh) - A simple yet delectable Roman pasta dish featuring pecorino cheese, black pepper, and a splash of the pasta's cooking water. A staple for those who appreciate traditional Italian cuisine.

- **Roma:** Spaghetti alla Carbonara (spah-geh-tee ahl-lah kahr-boh-nah-rah) - Comprising al dente spaghetti with a creamy sauce made from eggs, pecorino cheese, crispt pork cheek, and freshly ground black pepper. An indulgent must-try in Italy's capital.

- **Napoli:** Pizza Margherita (pee-tsah mahr-geh-ree-tah) - Hailing from the birthplace of pizza, it features tomato, mozzarella, basil, and olive oil. Uncomplicated and utterly flavorful.

- **Napoli:** Sfogliatella (sfoh-lyah-tehl-lah) - A Neapolitan pastry made with a flaky crust filled with ricotta cream or pastiera. A delightful treat for the senses.

- **Napoli:** Pastiera Napoletana (pah-styeh-rah nah-poh-leh-tah-nah) - A traditional Easter dessert from Naples, it's a fragrant, delicious pie made with a special crust filled with ricotta, cooked wheat, eggs, candied fruits, and orange blossom.

- **Firenze:** Bistecca alla Fiorentina (bee-steck-kah ahl-lah fyoh-ren-tee-nah) - A succulent grilled steak, typically served rare, which is a Florentine delicacy. Pair it with a glass of Chianti for the full Tuscan experience.

- **Venezia:** Risotto al Nero di Seppia (ree-zoh-toh ahl neh-roh dee sehp-pee-ah) - A unique Venetian squid ink risotto. Its dark color and sea flavor are unforgettable.

- **Milano:** Ossobuco con Risotto alla Milanese (ohs-soh-boo-koh kohn ree-zoh-toh ahl-lah mee-lah-neh-zeh) - Ossobuco is a slow-cooked veal shank with marrowbone, paired with saffron-enriched Milanese risotto, a Milanese classic.

- **Bologna:** Tagliatelle al Ragù (tah-lyah-tehl-leh ahl rah-goo) - Home-made tagliatelle with a meat sauce, known as ragù, an iconic dish of Bologna, distinct from the international version of 'spaghetti bolognese.'

- **Palermo:** Arancini (ah-rahn-chee-nee) - Sicilian rice balls, often filled with meat ragù, peas, and cheese. A tasty treat perfect for snacking on the go.
- **Genova:** Trofie al Pesto (troh-fee ahl pehs-toh) - Traditional Ligurian short pasta served with Genovese pesto, a sauce of basil, pine nuts, cheese, garlic, and olive oil.

- **Genova:** Focaccia Genovese (foh-kah-chah jeh-noh-veh-zeh) - A beloved Ligurian specialty, this thick and fluffy focaccia is seasoned with olive oil, sea salt, and occasionally onions or olives.

- **Catania:** Pasta alla Norma (pah-stah ahl-lah nor-mah) - A Sicilian dish of pasta with fried eggplants, tomato, salted ricotta, and fresh basil, named after the opera composer Vincenzo Bellini from Catania.

Famous Local Wines To Pair With The Most Famous Italian Dishes

- **Roma (Cacio e Pepe and Spaghetti alla Carbonara):**
    - Frascati (frah-ska-tee): A crisp and aromatic white wine from the Lazio region.
    - Cesanese del Piglio (cheh-zah-neh-zeh del pee-lyo): A red wine known for its red fruit and spicy notes, also from Lazio.

- **Napoli (Pizza Margherita):**
    - Lacrima Christi del Vesuvio (lah-kree-mah kree-stee del veh-su-vee-oh): A volcanic wine, either red or white, produced on the slopes of Mount Vesuvius. Known for its unique mineral notes and versatility.

- **Firenze (Bistecca alla Fiorentina):**
    - Chianti Classico (kee-ahn-tee klah-see-koh): Produced in the heart of Tuscany, this red wine is renowned for its red fruit profile and structured tannins.

- **Venezia (Risotto al Nero di Seppia):**

- Prosecco (proh-sehk-koh): One of Italy's most famous sparkling wines, fresh and effervescent, ideal for pairing with seafood.

- **Milano (Ossobuco con Risotto alla Milanese):**
    - Barolo (bah-roh-loh): A robust and structured red wine from Piedmont, often referred to as the "king of wines."

- **Bologna (Tagliatelle al Ragù):**
    - Sangiovese di Romagna (san-joh-veh-zeh dee roh-mahn-yah): A balanced red wine with notes of cherry and plum, typical from the Romagna region.

- **Palermo (Arancini):**
    - Nero d'Avola (neh-roh d'ah-voh-lah): A rich and full-bodied red from Sicily, known for its deep color and berry flavors.

Brief Guide To Italian Wines

- **Amarone della Valpolicella (ah-mah-roh-neh della val-poh-lee-chel-lah):** A dry red wine from the Veneto region, renowned for its rich and complex flavor with notes of dried fruit, plum, and spices. It's a luxurious choice for special occasions.

- **Barolo (bah-roh-loh):** Originating from the Piedmont region, Barolo is a red wine known for its strength and intricate flavor profile. It carries notes of red fruits, roses, and tar, often referred to as the "king of wines".

- **Barbaresco (bar-bah-res-koh):** Also from Piedmont, Barbaresco is akin to Barolo but tends to be a bit more approachable and less tannic. It boasts a rich flavor of red fruits and spices.

- **Chianti (kee-ahn-tee):** This Tuscan red wine is cherished for its versatility and fruity taste. It pairs wonderfully with a variety of Italian dishes, particularly those from Tuscany.

- **Brunello di Montalcino (broo-nel-loh dee mon-tal-chee-noh):** Another exquisite Tuscan wine, Brunello is celebrated for its depth and longevity. It offers a hearty flavor with hints of red fruit and spices.

- **Primitivo (pree-mee-tee-voh):** Hailing from Puglia, Primitivo is recognized for its luscious taste of black fruit and spices. It's a full-bodied wine and offers excellent value for its quality.

- **Nebbiolo (nehb-byoh-loh):** This grape variety is used to craft both Barolo and Barbaresco. It possesses an intricate flavor profile with hints of red fruit, spices, and roses.

- **Vermentino (ver-men-tee-noh):** A white wine produced in several Italian regions including Sardinia and Liguria. It has a refreshing, fruity palate, making it perfect for seafood and summer dishes.

- **Nero d'Avola (neh-roh d'ah-voh-lah):** This Sicilian red wine is celebrated for its flavors of dark fruit and spices. It's a popular choice to pair with Sicilian cuisine.
- **Gavi (gah-vee):** A light white wine crafted in the Piedmont region, Gavi is recognized for its crispness and flavors of green apple and citrus.

Useful Sentences When You Are At A Pizzeria

- **Can we have a table for four?**
    - Possiamo avere un tavolo per quattro? (pos-syah-moh ah-veh-reh oon tah-voh-loh per kwat-troh)

- **I'd like to order a pizza.**
    - Vorrei ordinare una pizza. (vor-ray or-dee-nah-reh oonah peet-sah)

- **What toppings do you have?**
    - Quali condimenti avete? (kwah-lee kon-dee-men-tee ah-veh-teh)

- **I'd like a Margherita.**
    - Vorrei una Margherita. (vor-ray oonah mar-gher-ee-tah)

- **Can I have a pizza with ham and mushrooms?**
    - Posso avere una pizza con prosciutto e funghi? (pohs-so ah-veh-reh oonah peet-sah kon pro-shoot-toh eh foon-ghee)

- **I'd like it without olives.**
    - La vorrei senza olive. (lah vor-ray sehn-zah oh-lee-veh)

- **Do you have a whole wheat crust?**
    - Avete la base di pizza integrale? (ah-veh-teh lah bah-seh dee peet-sah een-teh-grah-leh)

- **How big is the pizza?**
    - Quanto è grande la pizza? (kwahn-toh eh grahn-deh lah peet-sah)

- **I'd like a calzone, please.**
    - Vorrei un calzone, per favore. (vor-ray oon kal-tsoh-neh, per fah-voh-reh)

- **Is this a traditional Neapolitan pizza?**
    - È una pizza napoletana tradizionale? (eh oonah peet-sah nah-poh-leh-tah-nah trah-dee-tsyoh-nah-leh)

- **Can I have extra cheese?**
    - Posso avere più formaggio? (pohs-so ah-veh-reh pyoo for-mah-jyo)

- **I'd like it spicy.**
  La vorrei piccante. (lah vor-ray pee-kahn-teh)

- **Do you have gluten-free pizza?**
    - Avete pizza senza glutine? (ah-veh-teh peet-sah sehn-zah gloo-tee-neh)

- **How long will it take?**
    - Quanto tempo ci vorrà? (kwahn-toh tehm-poh chee vor-rah)

- **Is it wood-fired?**
    - È cotta nel forno a legna? (eh kot-tah nel for-noh ah leh-nyah)

- **Can I have a beer with my pizza?**
    - Posso avere una birra con la pizza? (pohs-so ah-veh-reh oonah beer-rah kon lah peet-sah)

- **Is the dough homemade?**
    - L'impasto è fatto in casa? (leem-pah-stoh eh fah-toh een kah-sah)

- **I'd like some garlic on it.**
    - Vorrei dell'aglio sopra. (vor-ray del-lahl-yoh soh-prah)

- **Can I get it to go?**
    - Posso prenderla da asporto? (pohs-so prehn-der-lah dah ah-spor-toh)

- **Do you offer vegan options?**
    - Offrite opzioni vegane (of-free-teh op-tsyoh-nee veh-gah-neh)

- **I'd like a slice of pizza, not a whole one.**
    - Vorrei una fetta di pizza, non una intera. (vor-ray oonah fet-tah dee peet-sah, non oonah een-teh-rah)

- **Do you have a family-size pizza?**
    - Avete una pizza familiare? (ah-veh-teh oonah peet-sah fah-mee-lyah-reh)

- **Is there a waiting time?**
    - C'è tempo di attesa? (cheh tehm-poh dee aht-teh-sah)

- **I'd like it well-cooked.**
    - La vorrei ben cotta. (lah vor-ray ben koh-tah)

- **What type of cheese do you use?**
    - Che tipo di formaggio usate? (keh tee-poh dee for-mah-jyo oo-sah-teh)

- **Can I pay by card?**
    - Posso pagare con carta? (pohs-so pah-gah-reh kon kahr-tah)

Useful Sentence Used By Italian Natives

- **A white pizza for me.**
    - Una pizza bianca per me. (without tomato sauce). (oonah peet-sah byahn-kah per meh)

- **I'd like some spicy oil.**
    - Vorrei un po' di olio piccante (vor-ray oon poh dee oh-lyoh pee-kahn-teh)

- **Could you bring me some chili on the side?**
    - Mi porti un po' di peperoncino a parte? (mee por-tee oon poh dee peh-peh-ron-chee-noh ah par-teh)

- **Better if it's not too cooked.**
    - Meglio se non è troppo cotta. (meh-lyoh seh non eh troh-ppoh koh-tah)

Brief Guide To Italian Pizzas

- **Margherita**: A base of tomato sauce, mozzarella, fresh basil, and extra virgin olive oil. It's said that its name comes from Queen Margherita of Savoy for the colors of the Italian flag: red (tomato), white (mozzarella), and green (basil).

- **Marinara**: Simple and delicious, made with tomato sauce, garlic, oregano, and extra virgin olive oil. Despite its name, it does not contain fish.

- **Quattro Stagioni**: Divided into four sections representing the seasons: black olives (winter), cooked ham (spring), mushrooms (autumn), and artichokes (summer).

- **Capricciosa**: A pizza with a combination of ingredients such as mushrooms, cooked ham, olives, artichokes, and mozzarella.

- **Diavola (or spicy)**: A pizza with a combination of ingredients such as mushrooms, cooked ham, olives, artichokes, and mozzarella.

- **Prosciutto e Funghi**: As the name suggests, this pizza is topped with cooked ham and mushrooms.

- **Quattro Formaggi**: A delicious combination of four types of cheese, often mozzarella, gorgonzola, fontina, and parmesan.

- **Napoletana (o puttanesca)**: Features anchovies, capers, and olives on a base of tomato sauce and mozzarella.
- **Bufalina**: Similar to Margherita, but made with buffalo mozzarella, a richer and creamier cheese.

- **Calzone**: Not exactly a pizza in the traditional sense, a calzone is a "half" pizza dough folded over itself, filled with ingredients like salami, ricotta, mozzarella, and tomato.

"Be aware, in Italy, pineapple on pizza doesn't really exist. You might find it in very touristy places to satisfy tourists, but in true pizzerias, we advise you not to order it!"

CHAPTER 8: NAVIGATING HEALTH IN ITALY

In this chapter, we'll tackle a topic that's important for any traveler—health. While we wish you a healthy and incident-free trip, it's wise to be prepared for the unexpected. We'll guide you through essential phrases for medical emergencies, understanding symptoms, and connecting with healthcare services in Italy.

The Italian healthcare system welcomes both EU and non-EU citizens in the case of emergencies. If you're from the EU, your European Health Insurance Card (EHIC) ensures you're fully covered in public hospitals. Private healthcare, however, requires immediate payment. Non-EU citizens, with mandatory health insurance for entry visas, are entitled to healthcare. Visit www.salute.gov.it for detailed information.

Now we'll go through useful phrases you might need when seeking medical help.

In case of an emergency, use "**Aiuto! Ho bisogno di un dottore!**" ("Help! I need a doctor") to call for help. Say "**Chiamate un ambulanza**" ("Call an ambulance") if you need an ambulance. To ask about nearby hospitals, use "C'è un ospedale qui vicino?" (Is there a hospital nearby?)

When in pain, it might be difficult to describe how we feel, especially if it's in another language. Here are some phrases you want to keep in mind.

- "Mi fa male": Used to express that you feel pain. For instance, "Mi fa male la testa" means "My head hurts."

- "Ho la febbre": If you feel feverish, use this sentence.

- "Mi sento debole": Say this sentence to communicate that you are feeling weak.

Locating healthcare facilities could be lifesaving, especially if you unexpectedly feel sick. Let's go through the names of some healthcare facilities.

- **Ambulatorio**: Visit an "ambulatorio" for non-emergency care and consultations. Most "ambulatori" offer a special service of medical assistance called **"Guardia Medica"**. It provides non-emergency healthcare during the hours when regular medical offices are closed. It is often available during evenings, nights, weekends, and holidays. However, just a few of them offer assistance for tourists, so you better look for **"Guardia Medica Turistica"** in the region you are in.

- **Pronto Soccorso**: It translates to the emergency room in English. For emergencies, say "Ho bisogno del pronto soccorso" to indicate you need the emergency room.

- **Farmacia**: Pharmacies offer over-the-counter medications and advice for minor illnesses.

- **Numero di Emergenza**: The emergency number in Italy is **112**, connecting you to police, fire, and medical assistance.

Finally, here is a simple figure which shows how to say in Italian some parts of the body.

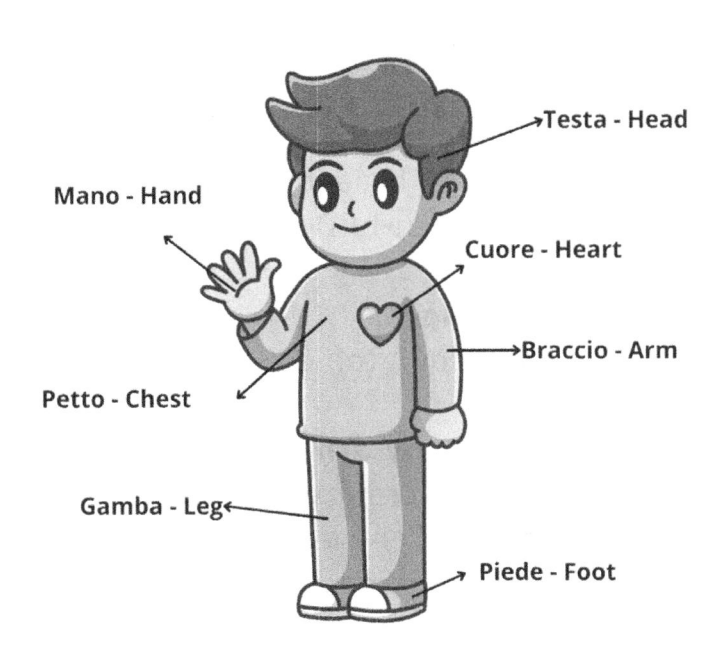

Testa - Head
Mano - Hand
Cuore - Heart
Braccio - Arm
Petto - Chest
Gamba - Leg
Piede - Foot

Now, you've equipped yourself with essential vocabulary for handling medical situations in Italy. While we hope you won't need these phrases, being prepared ensures a safer and more comfortable journey.

Useful Sentences

- **I'm feeling sick.**
    - Mi sento male. (mee sen-toh mah-leh)

- **Call an ambulance!**
    - Chiamate un'ambulanza! (kee-ah-mah-teh oon ahm-boo-lahn-tsah)

- **I've had an accident.**
    - Ho avuto un incidente. (oh ah-voo-toh oon een-chee-den-teh)

- **I have a pain here.**
    - Ho dolore qui. (oh doh-loh-reh kwee)

- **I think I broke my arm.**
    - Credo di essermi rotto il braccio. (kreh-doh dee es-ser-mee roht-toh eel brah-choh)

- **Where is the nearest hospital?**
    - Dov'è l'ospedale più vicino? (doh-veh lohs-peh-dah-leh pyoo vee-chee-noh)

- **Is there a pharmacy nearby?**
    - C'è una farmacia nelle vicinanze? (cheh oonah far-mah-chee-ah nel-leh vee-chee-nahn-tseh)

- **I'm allergic to...**
    - Sono allergico/a a... (soh-noh al-ler-gee-coh/ah ah)

- **Do you have this medication?**
    - Avete questo medicinale? (ah-veh-teh kweh-stoh meh-dee-chee-nah-leh)

- **I lost my medicine.**
    - Ho perso i miei farmaci. (oh pehr-soh ee myeh-ee far-mah-chee)

- **I need a prescription.**
    - Ho bisogno di una ricetta. (oh bee-zoh-nyoh dee oonah ree-chet-tah)

- **I feel faint.**
    - Mi sento svenire. (mee sen-toh sveh-nee-reh)

- **I can't breathe well.**
    - Non riesco a respirare bene. (non ree-es-coh ah reh-spee-rah-reh beh-neh)

- **I have a fever.**
    - Ho la febbre. (oh lah feb-breh)

- **I'm diabetic.**
    - Sono diabetico/a. (soh-noh dyah-beh-tee-coh/ah)

- **Can you help me?**
    - Puoi aiutarmi? (pwoy ah-yoo-tar-mee)

- **I need an emergency dentist.**
    - Ho bisogno di un dentista d'emergenza. (oh bee-zoh-nyoh dee oon den-teest-ah dem-er-jen-tsah)

- **Is it serious?**
    - È grave? (eh grah-veh)

- **How long will the treatment take?**
    - Quanto tempo ci vorrà per il trattamento? (kwan-toh tem-poh chee vor-rah per eel trat-tah-men-toh)

- **Do I need surgery?**
    - Ho bisogno di un intervento chirurgico? (oh bee-zoh-nyoh dee oon een-ter-ven-toh kee-roor-jee-coh)

- **Can you call my family?**
    - ○ Puoi chiamare la mia famiglia? (pwoy kee-ah-mah-reh lah mee-ah fah-meel-yah)

- **Where can I get medical supplies?**
    - ○ Dove posso trovare forniture mediche? (doh-veh pohs-soh troh-vah-reh for-nee-too-reh meh-dee-keh)

- **I need a doctor who speaks English.**
    - ○ Ho bisogno di un dottore che parli inglese. (oh bee-zoh-nyoh dee oon doht-toh-reh keh par-lee een-glay-zeh)

- **Can I see a specialist?**
    - ○ Posso vedere uno specialista? (pohs-soh veh-deh-reh oo-noh speh-chee-ah-lees-tah)

- **Is this covered by insurance?**
    - ○ È coperto dall'assicurazione? (eh koh-per-toh dal-lahs-see-koo-rah-tsyoh-ne)

- **Thank you for your help.**
    - ○ Grazie per il tuo aiuto. (grah-tsyeh per eel two oh ah-yoo-toh)

- **I have a medical emergency.**
    - ○ Ho una emergenza medica. (oh oonah eh-mer-jen-tsah meh-dee-kah)

- **Can I get a translator?**
    - Posso avere un traduttore? (pohs-soh ah-veh-reh oon trah-doo-toh-reh)

- **How much does this cost?**
    - Quanto costa questo? (kwan-toh koh-stah kweh-stoh)

Special And Customized Requests

- **I'm looking for the nearest ATM.**
    - Sto cercando il bancomat più vicino. (stoh cher-kahn-doh eel bahn-koh-maht pyoo vee-chee-noh)

- **Can you recommend a good local coffee shop?**
    - Puoi consigliarmi un buon bar locale? (pwoy kon-see-lyar-mee oon bwon bahr loh-kah-leh)

- **Is there a public restroom nearby?**
    - C'è un bagno pubblico nelle vicinanze? (cheh oon bahn-yoh poob-blee-ko nel-leh vee-chee-nahn-tseh)

- **I'm lost. Can you help me find my way back to [location]?**
    - Mi sono perso/a. Puoi aiutarmi a ritrovare la strada per [location]? (mee soh-noh pehr-soh/ah. pwoy ah-yoo-tar-mee ah ree-troh-vah-reh lah strah-dah pehr [location])

- **Is there a pharmacy open late at night?**
    - C'è una farmacia aperta fino a tardi? (cheh oo-nah far-mah-chee-ah ah-pair-tah feenoh ah tar-dee)

- **Can you recommend a good bookshop in the area?**
    - Puoi consigliarmi una buona libreria nella zona? (pwoy kon-see-lyar-mee oo-nah bwon-ah lee-breh-ree-ah nel-lah zoh-nah)

- **I need to buy a local SIM card.**
    - Devo comprare una scheda SIM locale. (deh-voh kom-prah-reh oo-nah skeh-dah seem loh-kah-leh)

- **Where can I find a post office?**
    - Dove posso trovare un ufficio postale? (doh-veh pohs-soh troh-vah-reh oon oof-fee-tsyoh poh-stah-leh)

- **Can you recommend a reliable taxi service?**
    - Puoi consigliare un servizio taxi affidabile? (pwoy kon-seelyar-eh oon sehr-vee-tsyoh tah-xee ah-feeh-dah-bee-leh)

- **Is there a local market open today?**
    - C'è un mercato locale aperto oggi? (cheh oon mehr-kah-toh loh-kah-leh ah-pair-toh oh-jee)

- **Can you help me with directions to the nearest train station?**
    - Puoi aiutarmi con le indicazioni per la stazione dei treni più vicina? (pwoy ah-yoo-tar-mee kohn leh een-dee-kah-tsyoh-nee pehr lah stah-tsyoh-neh dey trey-nee pyoo vee-chee-nah)

- **I need to exchange currency. Where is the nearest currency exchange?**
    - Devo cambiare valuta. Dove si trova la casa di cambio più vicina? (deh-voh kam-byah-reh vah-loo-tah. doh-veh see troh-vah lah kah-zah dee kam-byoh pyoo vee-chee-nah)

- **Is there a local gym or fitness center?**
    - C'è una palestra o centro fitness locale? (cheh oo-nah pah-leh-strah oh chen-troh feet-ness loh-kah-leh)

- **Can you recommend a good hiking trail in the area?**
    - Puoi consigliarmi un buon sentiero per escursioni nella zona? (pwoy kon-see-lyar-mee oon bwon sen-tyeh-roh pehr es-koo-zee-zee-oh-nee nel-lah zoh-nah)

- **Is there a local library where I can access the internet?**
    - C'è una biblioteca locale dove posso accedere a internet? (cheh oo-nah bee-blee-oh-teh-kah loh-kah-leh doh-veh pohs-soh ah-chess-seh-reh ah een-ter-net)

- **I'd like to rent a bicycle. Where can I find a bike rental service?**
    - Vorrei noleggiare una bicicletta. Dove posso trovare un servizio di noleggio biciclette? (vor-ray noh-lehd-jyah-reh oo-nah bee-chee-klet-tah. doh-veh pohs-soh troh-vah-reh oon sehr-vee-tsyoh dee noh-lehd-joh bee-chee-klet-teh)

- **Can you recommend a good local hair salon?**
    - Puoi consigliarmi un buon salone di parrucchiere locale? (pwoy kon-see-lyar-mee oon bwon sah-loh-neh dee pahr-roo-kyeh-reh loh-kah-leh)

- **I'm interested in local art. Can you suggest a good gallery to visit?**
    - Sono interessato/a all'arte locale. Puoi suggerire una buona galleria da visitare? (soh-noh een-ter-es-sah-toh/ah al-lahr-teh loh-kah-leh. pwoy soo-jeh-ree-reh oo-nah bwon-ah gal-lay-ree-ah dah vee-zee-tah-reh)

- **Is there a local cinema showing international films?**
    - C'è un cinema locale che proietta film internazionali? (cheh oo-n chee-nemah loh-kah-leh keh pro-yet-tah feelm een-ter-nah-tsyoh-nah-lee)

- **Can you recommend a good spot for bird watching?**
    - Puoi consigliarmi un buon posto per osservare gli uccelli? (pwoy kon-see-lyar-mee oon bwon poh-stoh pehr os-sehr-vah-reh lyee oo-chel-lee)

- **I'd like to explore local traditions. Are there any cultural events happening soon?**
    - Vorrei esplorare le tradizioni locali. Ci sono eventi culturali in programma presto? (vor-ray es-ploh-rah-reh leh trah-dee-tsyoh-nee loh-kah-lee. chee soh-noh eh-ven-tee kool-too-rah-lee een proh-gram-mah prehs-toh)

- **Is there a nearby beach or waterfront area?**
  - C'è una spiaggia o zona sul mare nelle vicinanze? (cheh oo-nah spee-ah-jah oh zoh-nah sool mah-reh nel-leh vee-chee-nahn-tseh)

- **Can you recommend a good local jazz club?**
  Puoi consigliarmi un buon club jazz locale? (pwoy kon-see-lyar-mee oon bwon kloob jazz loh-kah-leh)

- **I need to buy some local handicrafts. Where can I find a craft market?**
  - Devo comprare alcuni prodotti artigianali locali. Dove posso trovare un mercato dell'artigianato? (deh-voh kom-prah-reh ahl-koo-nee proh-doht-tee ar-tee-jah-nah-lee loh-kah-lee. doh-veh pohs-soh troh-vah-reh oon mehr-kah-toh del-lahr-tee-jah-na-toh)

- **Can you recommend a good local bar for live music?**
  - Puoi consigliarmi un buon bar locale per la musica dal vivo? (pwoy kon-see-lyar-mee oon bwon bahr loh-kah-leh pehr lah moo-zee-kah dal vee-vo)

- **I'm a photography enthusiast. Are there any scenic spots for photography in the area?**
    - Sono appassionato/a di fotografia. Ci sono luoghi panoramici per la fotografia nella zona? (soh-noh ah-pahs-syoh-nah-toh/ah dee fo-toh-grah-fee-ah. chee soh-noh loo-oh-gee pah-noh-rah-mee-chee pehr lah fo-toh-grah-fee-ah nel-lah zoh-nah)

- **Is there a local park with walking trails?**
    - C'è un parco locale con sentieri per passeggiare? (cheh oo-n par-koh loh-kah-leh kohn sen-tyeh-ree pehr pahs-seh-jyah-reh)

- **Can you recommend a good place to stargaze?**
    - Puoi consigliarmi un buon posto per osservare le stelle? (pwoy kon-see-lyar-mee oon bwon poh-stoh pehr os-sehr-vah-reh leh stel-leh)

- **Is there a local historical site with guided tours?**
    - C'è un sito storico locale con visite guidate? (cheh oo-n see-toh stoh-ree-koh loh-kah-leh kohn vee-zee-teh gwee-dah-teh)

Cultural Exchange:

- **What are some traditional Italian games or sports?**
    - Quali sono alcuni giochi o sport tradizionali italiani? (kwah-lee soh-noh ahl-koo-nee joh-kee oh sport trah-dee-tsyoh-nah-lee eet-ah-lyah-nee)

- **Tell me about the role of festivals and fairs in Italian communities.**
    - Parlami del ruolo dei festival e delle fiere nelle comunità italiane. (par-lah-mee del roo-oh-loh day feh-stee-vahl eh del-leh fee-eh-reh nel-leh koh-moo-nee-tah eet-ah-lyah-nee)

- **How do Italians typically spend their weekends?**
    - Come trascorrono tipicamente il weekend gli italiani? (koh-meh trah-skor-noh tee-pee-kah-men-teh eel wee-kend lyee eet-ah-lyah-nee)

- **What are some traditional Italian clothing items?**
    - Quali sono alcuni capi di abbigliamento tradizionali italiani? (kwah-lee soh-noh ahl-koo-nee kah-pee dee ahb-bee-glya-men-toh trah-dee-tsyoh-nah-lee eet-ah-lyah-nee)

- **Tell me about the role of family meals in Italian culture.**
    - Parlami del ruolo dei pasti in famiglia nella cultura italiana. (par-lah-mee del roo-oh-loh day pah-stee een fah-mee-lyah nel-lah kool-too-rah eet-ah-lyah-nee)

- **How is art incorporated into daily life in Italy?** Come viene incorporata l'arte nella vita quotidiana in Italia? (koh-meh vyeh-neh een-kor-poh-rah-tah lahr-teh nel-lah vee-tah kwoh-tee-dyah-nah een eet-ah-lyah)

- **Tell me about traditional Italian dance forms.**
    - Parlami delle forme tradizionali di danza italiana. (par-lah-mee del-leh fohr-meh trah-dee-tsyoh-nah-lee dee dahn-tsah eet-ah-lyah-nah)

- **How do Italians celebrate New Year's Eve?**
    - Come festeggiano gli italiani il Capodanno? (koh-meh feh-steh-jyah-noh lyee eet-ah-lyah-nee eel kah-poh-dahn-no)

- **What are some superstitions or beliefs in Italian culture?**
    - Quali sono alcune superstizioni o credenze nella cultura italiana? (kwah-lee soh-noh al-koo-neh sooh-per-stee-tsyoh-nee oh kre-dehn-tseh nel-lah kool-too-rah eet-ah-lyah-nee)

Special Chapter : Mastering the Basics

This special chapter is designed to equip you with fundamental elements for a smooth journey through Italy. We'll delve into aspects of the Italian language that are essential for everyday interactions. So, let's dive into the Italian alphabet, numbers, days of the week, months of the year, and the seasons.

The Italian Alphabet:

The Italian alphabet is similar to the English one, but a few distinctions make it unique. With 21 letters, excluding J, K, W, X, and Y, the pronunciation of certain letters differs. Understanding these nuances will aid you in spelling words and deciphering written information.

Italian Term	Pronunciation
A	[ah]
E	[eh]
I	[ee]
O	[oh]
U	[oo]
C	[cheh]
G	[je]
H	[ah-kkah]
Z	[tset-tah]

Seasons:

Knowing how to say the seasons of the year in Italian will guide you in packing appropriately for your Italian adventures, ensuring you're prepared for the forthcoming weather.

Season	Italian Term	Pronunciation
Spring	La Primavera	[lah pree-mah-veh-rah]
Summer	L'Estate	[leh-stah-teh]
Autumn/Fall	L'Autunno	[lau-toon-noh]
Winter	L'Inverno	[leen-vehr-noh]

Months of the Year:

To further assist you in planning, let's explore the months of the year in Italian. From Gennaio (January) to Dicembre (December), remembering these will prove invaluable when coordinating your visits to Italy and ensuring a well-organized itinerary.

Month	Italian Term	Pronunciation
January	Gennaio	[jen-nah-yoh]
February	Febbraio	[fehb-brah-yoh]
March	Marzo	[mar-tsoh]
April	Aprile	[ah-pree-leh]
May	Maggio	[mah-joh]
June	Giugno	[joo-nyoh]
July	Luglio	[loo-lyoh]
August	Agosto	[ah-gohs-toh]
September	Settembre	[set-tem-breh]
October	Ottobre	[oht-toh-breh]
November	Novembre	[noh-vem-breh]
December	Dicembre	[dee-chem-breh]

Days of the Week:

Planning activities and making reservations becomes more accessible when you know the days of the week in Italian. Understanding these terms will enhance your ability to schedule and organize your time effectively.

Day	Italian Term	Pronunciation
Monday	Lunedì	[loo-neh-dee]
Tuesday	Martedì	[mar-teh-dee]
Wednesday	Mercoledì	[mer-koh-leh-dee]
Thursday	Giovedì	[jo-veh-dee]
Friday	Venerdì	[veh-neh-dee]
Saturday	Sabato	[sah-bah-toh]
Sunday	Domenica	[doh-meh-nee-kah]

Numbers:

Knowing Italian numbers is crucial for various situations, from ordering your favorite pasta dish to understanding price tags. Let's start with the basics:

Number	Italian Term	Pronunciation
1	Uno	[oo-no]
2	Due	[doo-eh]
3	Tre	[treh]
4	Quattro	[kwah-troh]
5	Cinque	[cheen-kweh]
6	Sei	[say]
7	Sette	[set-teh]
8	Otto	[oht-toh]
9	Nove	[noh-veh]
10	Dieci	[dee-eh-chee]

You've now armed yourself with essential tools to navigate daily life in Italy. Whether you're exploring the vibrant streets of Rome, ordering a delicious gelato, or simply enjoying the beauty of the Italian countryside, these basics will make your journey more enjoyable.

Useful Sentences & Words

- **Tea**
    - Tè (teh)

- **Breakfast / Lunch / Dinner**
    - Colazione / Pranzo / Cena (koh-laht-zyoh-neh / prahn-tsaw / cheh-nah)

- **I don't understand**
    - Non capisco (non kah-pee-skoh)

- **Can you help me?**
    - Puoi aiutarmi? (pwoy ah-yoo-tar-mee)

- **I'm lost**
    - Mi sono perso/a (mee soh-noh pehr-soh/ah)

- **I need a doctor**
    - Ho bisogno di un medico (oh bee-zoh-nyoh dee oon meh-dee-koh)

- **Help**
    - Aiuto (ah-yoo-toh)

- **Emergency**
    - Emergenza (eh-mehr-jen-tsah)

- **Police**
    - Polizia (poh-leet-syah)

- **I'm not feeling well**
    - Non mi sento bene (non mee sehn-toh beh-neh)

- **Pharmacy**
    - Farmacia (fahr-mah-chyah)

- **How are you?**
    - Come stai? / Come va? (koh-meh sty / koh-meh vah)

- **I love you**
    - Ti amo (tee ah-moh)

- **What's your name?**
    - Come ti chiami? (koh-meh tee kyah-mee)

- **My name is...**
    - Mi chiamo... (mee kyah-moh)

- **Where are you from?**
    - Di dove sei? (dee doh-veh say)

- **I'm from...**
    - Sono di... (soh-noh dee)

- **Cheers!**
    - Salute! (sah-loo-teh)

- **Good luck!**
    - Buona fortuna! (bwoh-nah for-too-nah)

CONCLUSION: EMBRACING YOUR ITALIAN JOURNEY

As we reach the end of this guide crafted specifically for the average tourist like you, exploring the wonders of Italy, we genuinely hope this book has been more than a handy sidekick. Our aim was to equip you practically and to spark a newfound love for the diverse tapestry of Italian life.

Your journey through these pages is like a sneak peek into the adventures awaiting you in the lively streets of Florence, the bustling markets of Rome, and the serene landscapes of Tuscany. From learning how to greet people to handling medical hiccups with confidence, you've acquired some practical know-how for a more immersive experience.

As you dive into your Italian escapade, remember that beyond the language and traditions, the real treasures lie in genuine connections, shared laughs, and moments of awe. Italy isn't just about its historical wonders but also about the warmth of its people, the flavors of its food, and the timeless beauty that unfolds at every corner.

May this book be your trusty sidekick as you relish the taste of homemade pasta, marvel at the wonders of Renaissance art, and soak in the lively spirit of Italy. Whether you find yourself wandering the narrow paths of Venice or gazing at the grandeur of the Colosseum, let the essence of Italy capture your senses and make your travel tales unforgettable.

As you close this book, know that your adventure isn't confined to these words but is waiting to unravel in the charming squares, cozy eateries, and stunning landscapes that define Italy. So, go ahead, explore with curiosity, welcome the unknown, and let the enchantment of Italy unfold in ways only a journey can.

Buon viaggio e a presto!

This book is adapted from the video course "Italian Course for Travellers" by Italian House. Special thanks to Jasmine and the English House of Monteverde for their advice and creation.

By purchasing this book, you gain access to exclusive bonuses! Visit the web app at https://easyitalian.netlify.app or through the QR code below, using the code provided on **page 20.**

Through the app, you'll receive:
- The video course from which this book is adapted.
- The audiobook version of the course.
- The digital version of the book, available in both English and Spanish.

If you find this book helpful, we would be immensely grateful if you could leave us a review on Amazon, as your feedback is very important to us.

Lastly, don't forget to follow us on our active social media channels by searching for **italianhouse.rome** or **italianhouserome**.

Made in the USA
Monee, IL
23 February 2025